Wait 'Til You Have Real Problems

Wait 'Til You Have Real Problems

Poems

by Scott Beal

DZANC BOOKS

DZANC BOOKS

5220 Dexter Ann Arbor Rd.
Ann Arbor, MI 48103
www.dzancbooks.org

The characters and events in this book are fictitious. Any similarity to real persons, living or dead, is coincidental and not intended by the author.

Library of Congress Cataloging-in-Publication Data

Beal, Scott (Poet)
[Poems. Selections]
Wait til you have real problems : poems / by Scott Beal. -- First edition.
pages cm
Includes bibliographical references.
ISBN 978-1-938103-06-3
I. Title.
PS3602.E24293A6 2014
811'.6--dc23

2014039374

Published 2014 by Dzanc Books
Book design by Leslie Vedder

ISBN: 978-1-941531-81-5
First edition: November 2014

Printed in the United States of America

10 9 8 7 6 5 4 3 2 1

for Bill & Judi & Zoe & Jocelyn

"Dream of the Foam Toy Sword" appeared in Beloit Poetry Journal, 2014.

"To a Sports Talk Caller Who'd Refuse to Cheer a Gay Athlete Because 'I Just Don't Get It'" appeared in Southern Indiana Review, 2014.

"Chicken Soup" appeared in Prairie Schooner, 2014.

"Feats of Pain and Daring" appeared in Rattle, 2013.

"The Girl with Barbed Wire Hair" and "First Question" appeared in Union Station, 2013.

"The Snail Scene" appeared in Muzzle, 2013.

"Things to Think About" appeared in The Collagist, 2012.

"Elegy in Six Limericks" appeared in Radius, 2011.

"Bullet with Your Name on It" and "Assessment of My Masculinity" appeared in the anthology Unsquared: Ann Arbor Writers Unleash Their Edgiest Stories and Poems, published by 826michigan and The Neutral Zone, Ann Arbor, 2006.

"Falling Piano"; "Two Girls in a Georgia Cotton Mill"; "And then it hits you:"; and "Gross, Gorgonzola" appeared in Jangle the Threads, a split book with Rachel McKibbens and Aracelis Girmay, Red Beard Press, Ann Arbor, 2010.

"Two Girls in a Georgia Cotton Mill"; "Gross, Gorgonzola"; and "Watching My Daughter Learn to Skate at Veterans' Park" appeared online at AnnArbor.com.

"Things to Think About" was reprinted in Pushcart Prize XXXVIII: Best of the Small Presses, 2014.

"Things to Think About" and "Liner Notes" appeared in the anthology Uncommon Core: Contemporary Poems for Learning and Living, Red Beard Press, Ann Arbor, 2013.

Contents

fury tales

shade

pink air

where were you hit

fury tales

real problems

Wait ’Til You Have
Real Problems

fury tales

The Dream of the Foam Toy Sword

is as real as you, as real as the reign
of your inner confetti machine. The way you want
to be a real boy, a real seafood chef or arsonist, the way
you want to be a real housewife of Orange County
in the damp cellar of subcellular yen

is the way it wants to be a real sword,
to thicken its foam into devastating iron.
No more thwacks and thuds when it's parried
or bashes a plastic greave, it wants to clear
its molten throat and sing like a smithy,
it wants to strike the wall and gouge the brick,

it wants in the midst of the child's roaring
to swing its truest self, sudden steel, a new dense weight
dragging its arc toward the floor where it will slice right
and proper through a foot, hack it clean at the ankle,
no soft whump of an imminent bruise, no
chuckling dance of ouches but the godawful shock

of a lopped limb, of the world that ended
at the floor coming to end some inches above.
The sword aches to catalyze, to cauterize, aches
to inhabit its form and forge, its history
and factory of heat and blood and siege engines
the way you yearn to make yourself

a staggering lover or salesman-of-the-month
or half the father your father was, how
you churn your guts and wring your fists
to sift a cure for failure—just this deeply
the sword knows if its dream coheres, if it channels
the current racing down the child's arm,

the capillary hum and the lactic acid choiring
to the muscles, *burn, burn*, the lungs' shuffle
that feeds the child's vision of paladin, assassin,
if the sword's dream meets the child's as far
as the wrist that it could turn, that it can turn itself
into the dream and bite through birth and dawn.

CHICKEN SOUP

—for Joanna Ruth Bock

Instead of your soup I picked us up
a six-pack to split. But since you're six hundred
miles away I guess I'll drink yours too and hope
you catch a vicarious buzz through the poem.
Here's to your health. I'm trying
to make this warm and easy on the throat.
Fun fact: did you know that chicken noodle
soup was invented in the late Middle Ages
by a Benedictine abbess named Maria
della Fabriano when she tripped and dropped
the roasted chicken for the All Saints' Day
Feast into the bathwater of Sister Francesca?
And what, you may ask, would such a crucial
roast chicken be doing so close
to Francesca's bathing quarters? History
suspects the aroma was so intense
that Mother Maria could not resist
spiriting it directly to give her lover
a sniff. Imagine their faces,
pressed close—as Medieval nuns,
remember, they might eat
fresh meat twice a year in flush times—
imagine them leaning in, eyes half-closed,
both their faces aglow in the heat from the flesh

just pulled from the fire, and then the splash
as it slips from the platter into the tiny
tub where Francesca soaks. Imagine
the bird bumping warm against her skin,
waves brimming the edge of the tub
as she madly pulls herself up and out
to shiver naked at Maria's side as they both
stare down at the floating corpse of the abbey's
holy meal. Oh, they're screwed. So screwed.
And each on her own has already learned
to accept the probability of Hell,
but neither is willing to abandon the other
to damnation, not to mention expulsion
from the abbey and likely death on the streets,
so they hatch a crazy plan, and haul the tub
back to the kitchen, chop vegetables,
throw in strips of dough, and ladle it into bowls
for every sister at the feast, and for the visiting monks
from the next friary who've come to oversee
the proceedings. Mother Maria calls it divine
inspiration, this new dish, and every holy personage
in the hall gulps down spoonfuls of Sister Francesca's
bathwater, her first bath in weeks, and all pronounce
the soup delicious, and give thanks in prayer, and Maria
and Francesca are saved, and go to Heaven,
where they are now, I promise, could anyone
make up a story like this?

Falling Piano

A man presses a gun to his lover's head
and it's going to go off. They both know it,
and the man sees that soon as the bullet leaves
the barrel he'll wish it back, he'll bend
all the magnetism in his skin to call it back
and it won't come. The piano
has been falling for hours. Inside
a small girl crouches. It's been falling
for days, has long since stopped
accelerating so she feels it's safe to climb out,
props the lid and the updraft gust
points her braids at stars. They're so far above now
she can't remember if she fell from heaven
or a shuttle colony of rich eccentrics,
but either way she wonders if their music
has ceased, if revelers in gowns and tuxes
bend silently over a hole to watch the piano's
dark curves dwindle, or if they simply
roll other instruments from the wings
and go on waltzing. The man can see
how the bullet will take apart the head
and how he will want it whole again, but he is
so angry at what the brain inside must be
thinking of him, his heart can't stop
his fist from squeezing. The piano
scatters flocks which reform in its wake

and dives through radio waves that carry
sonatas to far antennas without stirring
its strings. It has fallen for years,
the girl's grandparents are dead, her parents
wouldn't know her face. The earth rises
to meet her and on it the man can see
there'll be nothing left but to turn the barrel around,
the girl on the piano flails at keys, a pilot
desperate to eject, notes trickle to the man
and his lover, some atonal nightmare surging
toward its crowd, crescendo, crash.

Two Girls in a Georgia Cotton Mill

—after a 1909 photograph by Lewis Wickes Hine

I have such a crush. Girl on the left
full of a laugh she barely holds in,
frumpy dress and braids be damned.
I'm in love with the tattered jacket
of the girl on the right, her chaos of hair,
that smile like she's seen a bird hatch
from a hand, pleased as if youth
could shrug off the teeth of the machinery
aligned behind her, eating up the frame,
the promise of her life, six days dawn
to dusk 'til never. The photo hides
the stench and heat, freezes the light
before afternoon thins into three feet of dark
between brick and steel, leaves out
the promise of beatings, pennies of pay
to barely keep them eating.
This lucky moment, the smiles despite,
that's what ruins me about history, that joy,
those sparks it falls over like a bell
built to smother. Yank them free,
pack knapsacks with sandwiches,
shove them on a yellow bus. Keep them
from blurring like the ghost
of the woman who rises behind them.

The Girl With Barbed Wire Hair

The man rips back a fistful of her hair
and it flares into barbs.

Like that, his fist shreds. She dashes
but his screams ring

the alley with no doppler
downshift, she flees at the speed of normal panic

while his left hand cradles his wrecked right:
last fist it'll ever make

to raise for breakaways
or saviors, to clutch a fork

or forge a check, offer a balloon to a child
or teach its mother a lesson. These things

shouldn't happen, but here she is next week
leaning into her school locker,

barbed hair snagged in the vents.
It occurs to kids who pass that they could help

but they're terrified to touch her.
She wonders herself

about contagion, never trusts
the blood she shampoos each morning

from her scalp. She learns to sleep
light, balanced gently on the pillow

and her neck grows oddly muscled from this posture
as its skin thickens, coarsens.

She wonders why barbed wire?
Why didn't her hair turn asps or blaze

but in the asking she knows, pictures
a huge pink bunny on whose lap

her mom once sat her at the mall, the hard clod
digging into her leg. Glaring back

into its plastic face, she'd found
two eyes burning between the smiling lips

and thought of the lust of rabbits, the greed
of rabbits who ravish gardens in tales,

against whom farmers raise sharp fences.
But the man in the alley wore no mask.

Bitch he'd spat
as he grabbed for the head she'd dared

to turn away, and *bitch* again
as he crouched over the flesh

she'd wrecked, as if she could command
all the iron in her blood to rush

to her split ends and steel into thorns.
Though the resulting anemia would explain a lot—

a blanched complexion people come to read
as goth, the midday faintness that bids her bend

her head against the locker
from which finally she comes unpinned.

Inside she finds a comic left
for her, *X-Men # 171*, with a startled heroine

circled on the cover, and flipping through
she finds this woman

is death to touch, drains soul and force
at the slightest brush of skin,

a power the hero cannot alter
and did not choose. The girl understands:

she has no magic, her hair is fixed
in these barbs, she'll never sprout

new limbs or blade her tongue:
the agency was his. Where did he get it,

this power? Who else has felt it?
Her eyes dart for signs

but the man is nowhere. Is
everywhere. It takes practice not to flinch

from a handshake. That's her story,
and though wishing is impotent,

I'd never wish it on anyone. But I'd wish it
for a friend's sister, grabbed at eleven.

I'd wish it for a niece
who had no hidden spines or quills

to ward away her stepfather's fingers.
I wish it for her voice

to flash forth and bind him in wire
though it dredge her marrow to speak.

Woman Gives Birth to Baby Made of Cork!

And—surprise!—it's not expected to live. And—surprise!
—the woman's to blame: too much fiber, or so much wine
her body built a stopper, or sex
she should know better than. Heads are demanding
blood tests and charges and reparations
to taxpayers. Their hooks find her
here, through waiting room televisions,
yank her bit by bit
toward the howling ether, even in these moments

after the doctors have pried her baby
from her arms and whisked it to a table
for procedures she doesn't understand
any less than they do. The hooks find her
through clinical echoes
explaining this may be her last touch
of skin that isn't
skin but feels soft and responsive,
its face carved in her likeness. Her body built

a stopper, they say, then pushed it
out, and now nothing stops, however tightly
she coils, nothing in her body stops roiling
under the skin she feels
tug from her bone like it's bubbling.

Nothing in it stops hollering for that genie that never
in nine months kicked, but rolled gently against
the upper edge of the amniotic sac,
being built to float. Being built to rise.

shade

ROUTINE ULTRASOUND

Twins now—how to manage that? How slake and taxi and
homeschool
four at once, how spend the extra as Leo scrapes? But love
brings them around as it has to. If there's an intelligence in
our designs
it's that our brains and hearts are primed to hash it out, one
dragging
the other until both believe in what must be done:
shave the 'stache, drown the cats. They go gushy for the
twin clumps
asserting into parallel skins, parallel nerve mazes.
Marcie swells and prays. She's grown up snapping to
Christian Contemporary,
warmed by a conviction in saviorship. Everything is going to
be fine.
A routine ultrasound shows a hole in one twin's heart. It's
dangerous
for both. The one, only a miracle could see born alive.
One chance in millions to make six months. They name her
Elizabeth—
consecrated to God: she'll be a living testament to grace
or join it straight in Heaven. But the longer she lives, the more
energy starved from Marcie's body, the worse for Abigail,
the other
twin: statistics insist if Elizabeth lives to birth she'll kill
them both.

This is the knowledge that steeps into Marcie's tissue, the
weight
she must carry to term. One lives, both die. What
can she pray for?

First Service at Bedford Nazarene

The Ark had a rollover accident and we're trapped
in the cavern of its hull: warm wood beams

curve to the inverted V of the vault, and perpendicular planks
frame the ceiling. The girl behind us starts to sob.

Some of us are not right with God. For over an hour,
the priest's been calling us forth to kneel and commend

ourselves to the local cross. CJ and I cling
to our seats: not pews, but interlocked,

green-cushioned chairs. Some of us are wrong
with God. The weeper is Marcie,

nineteen, not yet married or mother, seated between
her parents at whose urging we're here.

When I say the priest calls us forward I mean
CJ and me. We've been expected. We've been had.

No other hurries to the altar, though the voice wrings
the nave past all patience, because they know

what he knows: that we the guests are not
right with God. I scan the ceiling for a gap

to wedge between planks, a grip where God
could twist one rib from the vault to build a companion church

next door and drop us there. Overhead I find brass and glass,
a chandelier of concentric panes

like a drill of light boring toward my skull. As the priest persists
I feel it unscrew me from my seat,

extract me like a bad tooth
to be replaced with enamel in another's image—

I harden in my seat and behind me
a girl who loves me who hardly knows me,

like a savior, is stumped.

HALF-LIFE

The way balancing loaded plates my arms spazz
and splatter the patio with melon and beans, I'll
see the baby I cradle at the top of the stairs
drop over the rail, turn through slow air,
quiet, a loose sack of rags, and smash
two steps from bottom. I feel the hole
in my arms where the baby had been and the reel
of the future spools away, rushing down
the flight, pleading with the sack to stop
spilling, and the call to the pointless ambulance,
fingers struggling for the numbers to call
my wife, my lungs creaking like a spring
and the inconceivable act of hanging up the phone
after, its tiny click snapping me in half
at the top of the stairs, where I stand holding
a sleeping child in perfect calm, staggered.
This is my half-life of imaginary impulses,
in which every knife in my kitchen has filleted
the arm of my daughter then fallen from my grip,
then brooks of blood, sirens and cuffs
and worthless, whispered apologies for what
I can't imagine I could have done. I can shake it.
I almost faint then I shake it and the baby is lain
calmly to sleep in the crib, and the chicken is trimmed
for dinner, cleaver and cutting board soaped and rinsed
and safely stored. I don't show a bruise

and neither does my girl, there is no wound,
no screams or scabs, there is no lesson
I can learn, no dose I can gulp to quell these glimpses.
Just useless closeness to terrible parallels
we hover a flinch from, a twitch from
pleading through the ceiling *undo undo what's done.*

Heliosphere

Though we owe it all to our bright white hole in the sky—

live feed from a throat of fire,
a quaking furnace—any old solar flare
concussive enough to rubble our continents—

this is not His gift to us. His gift to us

is distance, which turns cataclysmic force
to warmth, the water cycle, though even at billions
of arms' lengths, heatstroke too, melanoma, flash
fires—enough death to remind us
point blank, suns scourge.
Distance lets there be light.

Intensive Care

One twin born with a hole
          through the heart's inner wall
beyond all hope of building
          itself to health
or the girl's life past
          three antiseptic months—
tell me again what this has to do
          with grace.

Under secular fluorescence
          surgeons repair the botched septum
enough to unfasten her body
          from a complex of plastic
so the child may live
          some weeks of ordinary warmth
among shadows cast by sunlight
          before her Christmas funeral.

This daughter the mother names
          Elizabeth—*consecrated*—as if to answer
how much she is
          willing to concede in her belief
there is a loving plan that needs
          this pain; and belief recalls
that having slammed the sky
          on all his sons and daughters,

boiled the marrow in his bones,
God blesses Job at last with insight,
new children, and redoubled flocks
to leave them after long years;
and it's true Abigail, the other
twin, learns to breathe and grow,
true the mother has found
an edge of love difficult to know—

but when Job rises in the dark to tuck
skins around the shoulders
of each beloved new guest
born into his second life,
and stirs the hearth to warm
them until morning, if each brush against
coarse fur or cast iron
does not stoke a pit

in the depths of him to blaze
with a fresh curse for God
on behalf of each slain child
then to hell with Job.

SECOND SERVICE AT BEDFORD NAZARENE

Even before the priest's speech uncoils, we are shambled.
A child has died. We have heard a mother split grief into notes

and string her song over the congregation like a web,
shivering. We have heard

the slow tremolo of a father's voice describe
a certain striking brightness that was

in his child's eyes. We have felt his density
sink in waves beneath the gathered,

the surviving children, and bear them afloat,
against all the weight and wonder of a child

given and taken in a breath,
the hole gouged out of each of us,

and we are caught between wrack and balm.
There is nothing left to say save

what we might say in small, in the quiet of after.
But because it is his church, and the day after Christmas,

and not just the family but his entire flock has come
for service and sermon, the priest takes the podium.

I would not say his speaking snakes
between ribs and warps their latticework until the heart

juts through shells. I would not say I have sat with an earnest hope
as it has been chopped and boiled

and strained through the sieve of his
earnest hope. I would not say I have clutched my head and rocked

and prayed
that God would enter the house and close his throat—

before he insists
that God singled out this mother and this father

to suffer because their faith
is strong enough to stand it. You mongrel

and dunce. What could blunt your appetite
if you'll gorge on an infant's corpse,

if you'll order us forward even
now to kneel, not to fail

her by withholding the one gesture He sent
her death to extract? Can no plan of God unfold without

your bidding? I would say
what is sent by God appears as if by chance,

a dent in a wheel that never comes full circle,
whereas your plan is tidy, petty,

a miniature wheel with you at the hub
and far narrower than the pain

you deign to wind upon it—now
surging through mother and father,

blooming and branching
into a Leviathan you can't draw with a hook

only God can do that
and you do not lead him on a leash.

HALF-LIFE

There is no amnesia, no forgetting:
imagine driving nails
in the mantle for stockings—how many,
do you leave an empty nail where hers
should have hung, and when Christmas Eve
you fill them, with what do you fill
that space? When you buy
this twin an Easter gown, a graduation dress,
your shadow buys the matching dress.

Visions make impressions. Do you ever suspect,
as I have, they could be real? That we're a quiver
from a plane along which the unthinkable has happened,
or hasn't? And that arriving there would be simple,
as effortless as adjusting the light? Could you
scoot a little to the left? Just this once, God?
Is that what you pray for?

pink air

PINK A

Hester Prynne's blouse has spun
through the wash so often it flaps
from the line like a banner
for sissy anarchists.

What had been fire is icing,
deveined, blood-drained.
Boys kiss on the corner as a man
glares through drawn curtains,

not conscious of how their stark
stripes have softened to near
transparence, which is just
what sunlight does.

Pinkie

To make you spill your secret they chop
this finger first. It can only get worse,

the pinkie does squat—not point, not
snap, prop a gold band or tickle

a trigger. You won't miss it
'til you're back at the laptop trying to mind

your Ps & Qs, to backspace out of jams,
make margins move. You'll stretch

your phantom digit for the Shift
to layer other keys with options,

versions, and wish the pinkie's touch
had done the same for keys on chains, worked

fresh means on a lock or ignition
as the bullies were at your back—

the fist you have left might crack
a jack's jaw but it's all wrong to drum

a barred door.

PINKEYE

What do you mean, you have pinkeye?
What is this, kindergarten?
Don't you get that from swimming in pools kids pee in?
You can't tell me you're missing your shift
because you soaked your face in a vat of pee.
You're high, right? Tell me you're high.
Tell me you're having an allergic reaction
to your THC. No?
You pitched against an oak limb.
Veered into a doorjamb. Say your aunt
died. Say your dog died. A cue jumped
from an adjacent table, a seed
squirted from a sliced jalapeño. Tell me
you were peering into a drain
to find what spindly thing scuttled down it.
On second thought, make it your father who died
so at least I know
you had a man to raise you not
to let some punk kids piss in your face.

Pinko

  look out, she's gonna blow
a bugle or your cover or a candle out, o
  the lips' circumference in shame-

faced flush—she's gonna blow a lubricious
  kiss through a keyhole or
a tapped telephone—whisperweight,

  whistling away, o sympathy and sex
in quailing chorus—
  the give and gasp in the blush

in the midst of touch, o purse and gloss,
  the lung's hoop to leap through,
what girlish gush,

  a tidy trick that conspires in the dark
to sink ships and threaten spread,
  such soft levelings

against a neck, what terrible ways
  we yield—who could live
with such weakness—who wouldn't dig

up the crusading senator's skull
to bite it back, to make it face
the hollow fact

that all your soft and sweet
is a stretch over surface, a yawn
worth of purpose, and will pass.

PINK YOU

cosmetics aisle

Imagine unscrewing a bullet
on your own lips
for a kiss. No
dude, wait: imagine
tattoos you have to touch-up
every day. That's the price
of pretty: look like
you took a slap then turned
the other cheek.

candy aisle

You really gonna buy that
Bubble Yum? It's made
from radioactive erasers.
My sister popped
a pink cube in her
mouth and I watched
her tongue
swell from her lips
and balloon 'til it burst.

Barbie aisle

There's enough pink plastic here
to asphyxiate Godzilla.

Only one thing I've seen
in a magazine
was this pink and glossy.

I dare you to go in there.
There's no way I'm going in there.

Pink and Sometimes Why

This is just what sunlight does
to me: every bare inch to itchy blush.

It's not damage. It's not helpful
and I'm not being cute or sentimental,
got it?
My literal skin performs a kind of photosynthesis
got it?
and I froth pink as a strawberry shake.

You catch rays. I arrest them.
Deploy loratadine and factor forty-five.
At the pool I shine and smell like a Coppertone still.

I'm not being all goth or northern. I just can't
walk with you for long by the ocean.

Dear person I've only just met
again,
it's embarrassing how much I love you already—
if we could speak through screens of zinc oxide

but you're very bright
and I have to go inside.

where were you hit

Perseus in Reverse

I was a lucky kid. My first gift
was too good to open: a head
in a sack. No one would play with me,
so I talked to statues. When I thought
they whispered back, it was the gift,
hissing. I loosed the ribbon, clenched
the wriggle, and lifted. Only for a second.
I never saw the head, I was fixed
on the statues: stone ballooning pink
with gasp and pulse. Eyes brightening
in fury. These men were not
young. Imagine how it must feel to be
born at their age. I dashed
for an outbound ship. New to their limbs,
they couldn't catch up, so they turned
to hunt my mother.

I married the first girl I met. (I was
a stupid kid.) After the ceremony
she said I'd saved her. From her parents,
their debts, their bargains
with cruelty. She said I had given her
life. The way she put it made me think
of the gift. I heard it in its sack all night,
saw the walls seethe. Half dreaming,
I dragged my bride to the sea and clacked

irons on her arms. Fished a serpent
from the surf and left before I
or anyone could see what happened.

I came to the wailing island as if to
a gravity made to catch me.
Two hags with wings and scales
railed over a corpse. I reached in my sack
and produced my gift. They must have seen
a knot of snakes flash from the dead
thing's throat, then their whole sister
shudder in her sleep. They lay beside her.
Fleeing, I watched the three recede
in the mirror, dreaming of futures in which
they would be savage, farther futures
in which they would be ravishing.

I stumbled into a familiar hall—the place
I'd played as a child! And here
were the men who had been statues,
sloshing goblets. Their king toasted, told me
tomorrow he would marry my mother.
He asked if I brought a wedding gift.
He told me which one he wanted,
a head in a sack.

I promised it. I promised and found
my mother and told her everything.
Now we hide in a fisherman's cottage.
The stone men are furious at losing us twice.
My mother calls me her gift,

says we must trust our gifts to lead us.
So this morning we climb into a large black chest.
We shut ourselves under its lid.
We will ride the sea until we find
her father who was gone before I was born.
He was a difficult man, she says,
but he'd be crazy about me, I'd
knock him dead.

I Wonder Where Your Mother Is

my father said then decked me
and the world wrenched,

that's what I recall, not the smack
or ache of the blow but the swivel
of space before I found my head
90 degrees to the left,

and this was new, this was hard
to accommodate in my frame;
though I'd been spanked
enough for acting a shit, I'd not
been spun by a man's strength
across my face—

We stood a step through the door
of the hushed house, father and son
frozen under the ring of the words
I'd spoken, the detail omitted

so far from this telling, my *maybe*
in a tone which must have been
cheerful, as if eager for a surprise
around the corner, *maybe*—

I suspect my father heard hope
in it, and wish as I might I cannot
swear he did not hear
correctly, but no
weight was in me to moor
the words. I said them, *maybe*
she's dead

and all the earth yanked crooked and hung
out of joint, this I had done,
and though my mother
turned up folding a load of shirts
still warm into drawers,

the world won't straighten.

Oklahoma

The day we moved to Oklahoma the world
grew like a pocket map
opened out and smoothed wide.
The first morning I walked to school
my mom followed like a cartoon,
crouching at one bush, speed-
tiptoeing to the next. Tarantulas
big as a fist would show up
on your porch, or perched
on a baseball knocked down the street.
A tarantula taught you to wait.
When I romped with Dobermans
in my neighbor's basement, my mom
plucked ticks off my back with tweezers.
Each week she took me to play
checkers with old people.
When I let them win they'd gloat and sneer.
Neighborhood kids shot hoops
in my drive. In summer I'd let them
raid my fridge for Country Time in cans.
One day kids warned me that Dusty
was coming to kick my butt. I said, why?
They said, I don't know but he'll
smash your face. I'd been in Dusty's backyard
once, and a bug big as my foot
that looked like it was carrying pliers
made me scream like a kitten. Dusty rolled up

hulking on his Diamondback bike,
then every boy and girl for three blocks circled
as Dusty lumbered over to smack at my head.
I started smacking back and at some point
Dusty was on the ground and I stood
wondering, Is that it? But then a head
of frizzy curls bounded out,
as if I'd spat lead and dared all challengers,
and the crowd said Now you're dead—
Larry knows karate. Larry leaped over
with his fists up and we got our arms tangled,
then we were both down sweating
with his head locked under my arm,
and I started to feel strong, like everybody
wanted to take me out but no one could,
then a voice said You're choking him,
and I said No, it's a headlock,
and they said, Naw, cuz, you're choking him,
and I saw Larry's face looked hot
like the inside of a toaster. I wasn't ready to let go,
and then I let go, and rose,
and Larry gasped like a fish as he pulled himself up,
wheezing I'll kill you and calling me
things I'd never heard of as he chased me
around my neighbor's yard,
with everyone's faces hedging us in
as I dashed, not afraid of Larry or his alleged karate,
but of the shock of my hands, of the thing
I could have let them finish, and the map
folded under me with my mother inside it,
and there was no one to watch for me, no place to run.

The Medical Bay

I put my boy body into my friend's tub
and waited. I think that's how it went,
a dry tub, my clothed body, the thin sun
through the window and no one in the house,
all the boys shooting each other in the yard,
the memory is barely there, but yes laser fire,
yes crouching and chasing and imaginary

wounds opening as we rose up in front
of another boy's pointing finger. I don't
remember saying medical bay, or speaking
about technology or repair but when I think
how it happened, what gave me that giddiness,
it seemed we were aware of the need
to heal when we were wasted by the burn

of a laser strike to neck or thigh, and so
one would lie in what seemed the most restorative
space in the house, near our mothers'
gauze and peroxide, and wait.
When his absence was noticed, another
would find him and ask, where were you hit,
knowing seconds were precious, that their hand

was needed to bandage or magnetize
the wound back to health, I can't say

how we meant it to work or how it fit
in our hunt and blast system, but a laying
on of hands, here, Matthew, here is where
they got me, pointing to my crotch, I don't
remember if it happened, a touch

or the mere idea, I had no inkling what my body's
shape meant or where touch could take it,
and I wasn't afraid to say it, here, I wasn't ashamed
and I was, I knew it wasn't something to ask
on the battlefield. I'm only sure of the silence
in the tub and the warm patience
in my stomach, as if a loaf were rising there.

Assessment of My Masculinity

I have been drinking my coffee black
since the eleventh grade, my whiskey straight
since graduation. I have never killed anyone.
I did not, during the Gulf War, display
a flag decal in the window of my pickup.

I've never driven a pickup. I don't own
a hot car, or an uncommonly large penis,
and the one I have has not been
stuck into a vast array of girls.
I don't holler about those it has.

I have broken bones playing football,
long ago, not in high school, not on a team.
I never wore pads. I have
medical insurance. I have been drinking
my coffee black, my whiskey straight,

for years. I have never killed
anyone. I don't have any business
sense. I just write my goddamn poems,
but they are not just poems, they are
my goddamn poems. I stop

and ask directions. I have never
liked fishing. I have been drinking my coffee

black since the eleventh grade. This doesn't matter
until I tell you, man, and then
I am one of you, even though I have

never killed anyone. In primary school
I got battered. I didn't fight back.
One time, this guy knocked me down.
I got up, he knocked me down, a lot of times.
I only snickered at him, sore but

thinking I felt like a man.

SPOILER ALERT

Kid, I admit: all the roots of my never knowing what to do
I see in you. In zippered velour and lost contact lenses.
Every time you mustered the guts to risk humiliation
and got it in triplicate. It gets better, but you need to hear this.
I wince. When the redhead and her friend try not to laugh
as she shrugs, "Sorry." Then they laugh. That's what you get
when you write your biography in a check-box note signed

"Don't break my heart." The worst is the trying not.
They knew what laughter would do to you, but couldn't help it.
You were that pathetic. I think you have a right to know
a part of you will always be that pathetic.
Not some diseased and removable part like your appendix
or your tonsils (one of which you get to keep).

A vital organ. When you chase your jacket by the bike rack
as it helicopters from hand to hand. When you aren't sure
what fucking is but tell how you fucked your cousin
'cause she's the one pretty girl they don't know
would never talk to you. But listen: sex is a Rubik's Cube
you'll someday solve. It won't happen the way you imagine it
in bed when you're ten: two older girls abducting you

from the drive where you've been shooting hoops, then stashing
you naked in a basket suspended from a dark ceiling by ropes
while you wait to learn what they can do to your body. It may never

match that standard but you'll flush with the same shuddering.
As for the real Rubik's Cube, forget it. You'll never design fiends
for Gary Gygax or play searing leads for Dio. All your parents'
Winstons you flushed or ripped in half you'll one day wish

were lit in your left hand, even after Nanny dies, and Les dies,
and Dean dies of cancer, and your dad boils in dry ice
to be the first who doesn't. A whole bunch of sex and death
before you, kid. Remember how you swore to Christ
you'd never work in an office? You'll work in an office.
You'll temp. You'll fucking take dictation. You'll do
the devil's work and repair your credit rating. I guess

that's what they meant when they said Wait 'til you grow up
and have real problems. You were right to hate them
for saying that. Just live through this. This is the worst of it.
I could tell you Fred Schmidt grows up to be a sad, fat asshole
and that Rodney wears dentures and works at a bowling alley
and Shane shovels shit and Mike moved into his mother's
laundry room, but the truth is better. I don't know

or care what came of any of them. You go to bed every night
with a lightning-hot woman in a house you own, and if Fred Schmidt
torched it tomorrow a dozen friends would take you in.
No one makes you wear a tie or go to church. You never forget
not to tell your kids Because I said so. That, you never forget.
There's no sign anyone heard a single prayer.
When you quit praying the world doesn't get worse.

Liner Notes

Scott would like to thank God, Mom and Pop, my brother,
especially my brother hauling his forty-ton rig cross-country
like a band on tour, crowds roaring
for paperbacks and twelve-packs, the burdens of stardom,
home snagging his brain and unraveling his years over
the Interstate Highway System. Bless him
for surviving. Scott would like to thank God
but can't. How do you love "Love me
or else"? I mean, if someone did
invent artichoke hearts and diminished fifths, blow 'em
a kiss. Scott would like to thank loofahs, ragtime,
and any weekday without a cubicle. Scott would like
to thank someone for Creation but hymns are for chumps.

Engineered by: Explosions and coherences, by carbon
schmoozing epoch after epoch, workaholics and alcoholics,
knockouts and good geezers. Produced by: Sex.
Scott would like to thank sex. His tongue
and fingertips for knowing how to make skin squirm
the right ways. Scott would like to thank the idea
of my parents having sex, without which no Scott
and no brother traversing the great American cities
to unload at back-alley warehouses then move on
before the show. My brother the roadie.
My brother the roadie for pretzel rods and boxer briefs.
Scott hopes his folks still get busy in their sixties.

Thanks to the doctors who stitched up my brother's skull
and mother's ulcers. And to waffle irons,
humpback whales, Irish whiskey, Joss Whedon.
Scott is vocals, percussion, and turbulent nerves.

Scott exclusively uses Colgate Cavity Protection dentifrice.
Scott has little use for "exclusively uses." Be kind, yes,
but you can't be kind *exclusively*. Sometimes you're gonna
be a jerk. All rights reserved. Scott exclusively uses
self-deprecating irony to touch up his base coat of self-
deprecating anxiety. Wiseass Remarks appear courtesy
of aversion to earnestness. Lurking in the Back
appears courtesy of gangliness in motion. And drugs.
Scott thanks drugs that make skin smolder with cold
but killed Dad's cancer, drugs that keep my brother safe
around a razor. Awkward Silence appears courtesy of
statistics: so many dipshit sayings,
such rare bits of pith. Try hard not to look
like a chump and you never look like anything else.

Unauthorized duplication is strictly uncool.
Unauthorized duplication is how brothers drive brothers
nuts, shadowing and touching their stuff and acting big.
It's why an older brother stiffarms and highsteps
into distance, leaving a hole in the world
where the squirt's still stuck. Scott would like to thank
my brother for surviving because someone out there was made
the same but sees and suffers through different
filters. Bless this country he takes in through a windshield
spattered with bug guts. I wish I could
clean it, brother. I wish I could pray it clean.

STRANGER

The beast the boy sees has a name—okapi—but the boy
has no way of knowing this. He is like Westerners
prior to 1901, for whom such a creature couldn't exist—
but here it stands ten yards from him,
absurd deer of rust ending in garish zebra hindquarters,
horned head with batlike ears, as constructed as a manticore,
but standing at the edge of the lot

of the house his grandfather built in Blissfield, Michigan, alert
and ready to bolt into the Congolese rainforest which is nowhere
in sight. We must not speak yet of its tongue. Let us speak
of the yard, of stacked, chopped wood and zips of cable
rattling with clothespins between cast steel Ts.
Of trees and targets and the chimney with a black iron plate
set with hinges, a senseless door into sometime fire.

It is no kind of door the boy knows how to open in the chimney
or himself. He has only seen it closed. It is convenient
for games, a sci-fi keypad, an opaque window, a vertical
        home plate
for family bouts of wiffle ball. Let us speak of wiffle ball,
a game which may break out in this yard five times in his life,
when the right mix of uncles and cousins tips
into the outfield which ends at the lot's edge where the okapi

waits with its exquisite long tongue of which we will speak,
but not yet. The boy stands poised as the wiffle ball whistles

through a veering arc toward the fat red bat beaming from
his hands
to thwack it square and loop it over the heads of every relative. Or
into their hands. Or to slice the ball back into the brick
rise of the chimney. But these outcomes are failures of his dream,
which is to pound the ball beyond the bounds of sense,

because he conceives the man he wants to be as excess
and outstripping, as a mandate to crack the ball farther
than cousin Michelle or her father. He may once, or he may
never. It won't matter. What he imagines now as the proof
of potential within him will prove to be cobweb on firewood.
But the failures will last. He will see them as he wanders
into the yard
when the rest of the family has not come, and the house is lonely,

and he stands measuring in his muscles the distance from
the chimney
to the street beyond the pines, and beyond that, to the river
where his father's sure feet once cut a narrow path on skis,
to fields where his father once made things break
with a shoulder or a shovel, and farther beyond, to the school
half a country away which will call the boy back
to teams he can't make and fights he can't win,

and as he tries in his joints to feel his next and hardest swing,
the okapi is there. I don't blame you if you don't believe it,
but understand the boy doesn't know what an okapi is,
that he won't until he sees it years after in a National Geographic
or at the San Diego Zoo, so for now he might call it
demon horse, or lollygaggery, or stranger, and I won't say
he fathoms but that he begins to suspect

the universe makes creatures that are not fully this
or that, fully other or one. At first he flinches
toward the hand-built house of timber and brick,
the safety of firelight, a desk with paperweights
and a black vinyl swivel chair, the cloud of smoke
from his grandfather's pipe and father's cigarettes.
Toward roof and lock, voice and ear. But then the tongue,

the beast's purple tongue flares forth, a full foot of it, and
then, a full
two feet, darting around its face without sound—
without vocabulary—a tongue with no saying,
but (like the boy's tongue) a muscle, extending into eyes and nose
and the ears we have called batlike but which are simply huge
and pointy as pixies', as wrong-looking as anything
in this world. The tongue which is muscle uncoils and twirls

itself into these ears to clean them. It minds its business,
and it minds the boy's—the okapi too on taut nerves,
hoof on half-panic. It doesn't break into speech or song,
offer lessons or explanation, but only stands at the edge
of shadows, unnamed. The boy knows
there are men who'd fire a shell
into the heart of such a beast to prove

it had walked in their sight. He's seen spear and saber
hung on his grandfather's wall, souvenirs
from wars far away. He stands gazing
at the demon horse and licking his lips and the air
around his face fills with tongue, simian tongue,
his one small tongue and the stories it can tell
and the stories it can never tell.

fury tales

Feats of Pain and Daring

Once I got lost alone in the woods
and found my way back. It made me
not new or strong, but wary of woods.
I trudged through shallow swamp and thickets
of prickers and chiggers, through tree dark
stretching all directions, four hungry hours
and no one made me do it the way they make you
chug a beer through a mouthful of tampons,
or get your bloody back daggered into crocodile skin,
or spill over the side of a bark canoe
and swim the quaking mile to shore.
No one spun me with a blindfold and basket
and said, Bear this back to the house of your father
and he'll pull the ripcord to rev your testicles
and carve you a sharp new Adam's apple,
no tribe had gathered to cheer as I stumbled
clear of the canopy and back into my prescription
for Clearasil, my graph paper dungeon maps.
This was before I failed to swing back at bullies,
before the summer I failed driver's ed
and took a makeup course at Sears
from a man who wore black socks with sandals.
It was not the woods where Wayne
led me to a Hefty bag of Penthouses and Hustlers,
their centerfolds stiff from snow. Not the woods
where Lee would stash a six-pack of beer

and a box of stogies in wait for me, and slowly finish
two of each as I stood refusing
to join him in fear of what my mother
would think. Last week I sat to watch
a National Geographic special with my daughter,
and the screen filled with a million shimmering sperm,
like Hubble footage of a skyful of galaxies
thrashing their little flagella to race
at a tenth of an inch per minute
through vaginaland. I said, You have to learn
about this stuff sometime, and she said,
No I don't. She's eleven. At her age I was abusing
a St. Louis Cardinals wristband so early
and often I never had a wet dream. We stopped
the film before one brave sperm could ignite
an egg into a person who would grow to the age
when they saw off your clitoris, or file your teeth
to points with a sharpened stone, or knit leaves
into a glove and fill it with bullet ants and watch
to see if you scream as you shove
your budding warrior hand inside. They make you breathe
in a burqa, stuff your foot into glass, volt you up
on brown-brown and hand you a machete. They offer
a doctored passport and a waitress shift in London
where you find yourself bound to a box spring
in a curtained corner. They want to test you,
they want to hurt you, they want to escort you
into the savage mess they've made of womanhood
and manhood. I failed in so many ways, I
was so lucky. I walked into woods by choice,
for kicks, it wasn't supposed to smelt me into iron

and it didn't. I even lied when I said I was alone.
I was with Greg Jensen, a boy I neither loved
nor respected, which made the loneliness worse
as we trod between wolf-whispering trees,
stomach-weak, scratched with brambles.
We had to hide the cowering boys inside us
and pretend we could hack it like men
who could swallow poison, take or give
a whip without flinching, like men who'd earned our way
to one day look a child in the face and say this
is how you grow up, this is how you die.

Caller Reports Baby in the Middle of the Road

She's old enough to stumble like a drunk. But she's got
  no shoes,
stamping through the gutter's burnt butts
and twisted lids. Babies always look dizzy, don't they,
can't keep a straight line, slur their sounds. Something's wrong
in their heads, they drool, you have to spoon them their food.
Wait, that's not a baby, that's a nine month old Jack
Russell Terrier with a limp. A cutie, even with the blood
shining on his coat as he spirals at the end
of my driveway, even with the man standing over him yelling
and holding a hammer. Ever notice how a hammer looks
  like a bullet
on a stick? I mean, sure, if you've ever been mad,
like a big bullet lollipop, they should make candy tools,
they'd be a huge hit, but yeah, the man
is swinging it behind his head, and that *is* a baby,
I'm so nearsighted, that dog's just a story
I read in the paper, and the man. And the hammer, it's
  the bumper
of a cruiser arcing slowly toward the next intersection
with clumsy pedestrians—no officer, by cruiser
I meant one of those crummy Chryslers that look like hot rods
for soccer moms. What kind of mom drives
past a baby in the street? That's a real story,
about the dog and the hammer, even if it's not this story, people

take out the little small part of themselves they hate, set it
down in front of them, and whack it with a hammer, their
private piñata
of shame and rage, only every time they hit it, it gets bigger,
it whimpers and won't stay in place, bites back or limps away
and has to be dragged by the tail, and you're heaving with
the strain
and the stains get on everything and the place inside you
where it sat
is so gouged out and blank that one siren, one phone call
folds you in.
Baby's finally fallen and started crying,
not like a person, like a full blast broadcast, like a loop delay
because someone always comes when she cries but no one
is picking her up.
I think you should send someone over. I think in one of
these houses
folks are opening cupboards, folks are shining
a flashlight down the basement steps, and calling a
beautiful name,
here Keisha, here Normandy, what have you gotten into now,
while in their heads it's fuck fuck fuck. Someone's side door
hangs a little open, they haven't yet spotted the moat
of light surrounding it though part of their brain
thinks it's funny that the minute the baby goes quiet
the idiots down the street can't shut their kid up.

Rapunzel's Contractor

Some ornate obelisk thrust above the canopy—
everybody's gonna wanna know
what that's about. So what we did, we converted
an old grain elevator—
our midwestern towers no one sees for seeing.

Behind every dark purpose lies a darker
need. Many bodies piled
to stoke a tiny, private furnace. I'd like to say I relied
on the check, my son would starve—that's why. But a secret
is a secret delight. I always felt the universe

was driven by vicious machinery, and now
I'd leaned close enough to grease a wheel. The child's bed
we raised with cranes, the dollhouse
with its working windows and doors
the tower had none of—well, we did add

one. Where else to lead in guests?
Once a man steps into a room like that
he never steps all the way out; wherever he stands
there's a corner
where his kick cowers under a sheet.

You heard what happened after. They say the hair
keeps growing after you die. Where did that prince

mean to climb? What did he think
to carry back? But here’s to happy endings
and healthy twins. Repeat business.

The Betties

> *"BRASILIA, Brazil — The stepfather of a 2-year-old boy found with 42 sewing needles in his body confessed to jabbing them into the toddler during a month of rituals with a lover who he claimed received instructions through trances, Brazilian police said Thursday."*
>
> —*Associated Press, Dec. 17, 2009*

> *"CHARLOTTE, N.C. — Cincinnati Bengals receiver Chris Henry has died, one day after falling out of the back of a pickup truck in what authorities described as a domestic dispute with his fiancée."*
>
> —*ESPN.com, Dec. 17, 2009*

We don't know what went on in that truck,
the local host says—the local host
says there's something about dames,
isn't there, that has the power

to raise your rage like no other thing.
One receiver's dead in the road

and his superstar partner's crying
because a latticework of needles moves in his body no
because his friend had faltered
but tightened his stride and "was
doing everything right."

In sixth-grade science I fainted over a girl's speech
on tourniquets. I've dropped

in a beachside shop at one red bead
where a shark tooth pricked
a fingertip. I've come to in bathrooms
all prickles and sunspots and not known
if my brain was mine, as we don't
know what went on in that truck
and a latticework of needles

moves in the body of a Brazilian boy.
Forty-two needles. One in a lung,
two near the heart, many spread
throughout the trunk, silver needles,
sewing needles, but pressed in one by one
by a bricklayer's hand—
            their placements, surgeons say,
so delicate and dangerous
removal may only cause more harm. He'll only survive
by growing around them. One receiver's crying

because another's dead in the road
and "he was doing everything right."
"He's beating on the back
of this truck window," said the 911 caller

and then he wasn't—

In a boy in Brazil are forty-two needles
pushed in by his stepfather,
whose lover had them blessed by a priestess
then directed their placements
from the distance of trances—this rite, he

said she said, would stitch them together—
this rite, police said, was pure invention, pure

vengeance: this is what women do
to men—this is what women make
men do
to themselves
the local host says

to his parasites in radioland
who despite where their knuckles and fathers' belts have been
soak up a victim narrative
of divorce attorneys for men
every ad break. We don't know what
went on in that truck,
what she was driving away with, or from,

just as I don't understand the biophysics
in a panther's skull or a slingback pump—
though I know the way
these bones have snapped and fused is built
into every goodbye wave
and a history of hurts

and backlash slurs are the granules around
which my tissues have grown, knots
the local host reaches to knock

by muscle memory, the way a receiver
after a turnover chases down the defender
driving away with the ball—

he's drilled
never to give up a score

and a boy in Brazil will grow with forty-two
needles forested within him.
Icicles and lightning. Mazed
and blessed and in his body. He'll live

with the pursuits they nettle him into
long after he forgets to feel
how their angles against his organs
threaten to spill out all that breath and bile.

Lip Gloss

The dame was never gonna love him. So we swigged
and cursed the skirt, the soft

pouting strumpet, we talked like that, we had a whole
litany and it was a joke but not joke
enough. The brain's a fizzy instrument

in the night's open lab, on the sidewalk
under a curtained window, where the green glint

of a bottle under the streetlamp
becomes a shatter
that can happen outside us. I persuade myself

I was just as drunk, I couldn't tell the bottle's lip
(like her lip) would not soften for him,

but was chipped sharp, that the neck that raised it
beneath his foot was (like her neck)
too firm to buckle to his boyish pressure,

but would pierce his boot and artery.
I insist I could not have swatted the bottle

or shoved him mid-stomp
to spare him that sickening hollowing and months
on crutches because I believed in it:

we'd been scorned men. One empty vessel
had to splinter and spread.

To a Sports Talk Caller Who'd Refuse to Cheer a Gay Athlete Because "I Just Don't Get It"

I get it—cocks are ugly,
all wrinkled pink blunt with veins,
not to mention the slit, not to mention
the balls spindly with steel wool wires.
I'm not particularly proud
to have one either, as you must not be
able to look at your own
without nausea and a shameful knot
exploding in your gut if you can't
imagine another man
turning his breath toward it.
How jagged that image inside
your skull, when the body
you watch sweating it out
on the court, the muscles you admire
rippling from the hands on the rim
to the chest beating full of triumphant fire
you too feel from your seat in the stands—
to think of that man
in a dark not far from you
holding another man, their embrace
that leaves you out,
giving each other something
you just don't get.

The Snail Scene

Mrs. Snail drags her gut over grass,
leaving a wake of slick bent stalks as she inches
toward the clearing where Mr. Snail lingers
to greet her. It takes forever
to arrive at the moment, and once there
they ripple in it, press
and press—more naked than naked,
glistening pink organs with calcite coils
slung on their backs. How
could those cups contain such extravagant
bodies? Waves of craving
pass through the seam where they're suctioned
close. Eyestalks curl and probe,
gazing with whatever awareness
snails gaze with—though to us
neither looks more butch than the other,
nor lovelier; we can't tell Mr. from Mrs.
because they both
are both. One's head leans into the other,
then tips back yielding—rapturous,
scandalous. How can any beast
touch so lushly? As if you were wholly tongue
and I was wholly tongue,
and the shells of our mouths hung to the side
as we shoved bud to bud.
As if we both could slide from under
our spiraling worlds,
pour skin to skin, and swim.

Beauty's Father

One comes upon it by unhappy wandering—that brambly castle where she lives. Nightly feasts are lit by low candles so every decanter throws long shadows. The tines raised over her plate become spectral blades raking her face. She is named well but won't believe it, and being a child she is careless and clumsy. She has seen my shoulders tighten as I sopped coffee she kicked over, heard me shout at the window she's opened to mosquitoes. She has shown me her poem about the five talking fish only to find my finger pointing to the numeral 5 written backwards. I did not know I was piling the walls stone by stone. I did not know I was building the beast in my own image, or how they would inhabit one another's reflections. That he would look on her and see the perfect fairness with which she'd been treated. That she would look on him and see her every failure twisting his face.

Beauty

all this food he pushes new dishes each night
like my dad but they're weird I bite a fruit
and it's spicy or a celery and it's gooey
so I hold out for a turkey dog cut in eight pieces
and bowl of shells and cheese, milk with vanilla
even that in a glass that'll break if I breathe
plates with swirly edges and so thin they shiver
when I clink my fork and odd shaped
dishes all over the table he says their names
and they don't make sense like one's a boat
but it's full of liquid so it must be
a bad boat and I'm like that, a boat with the sea
inside it so I can never get away. I eat slow
as I can, I get up and walk
around the table out of the room and up
and down the stairs which drove Dad
nuts but he never says a word just waits
at his end of the table an hour two hours
until my last bite and that's when he opens
his huge mouth of bent screws and the black
tongue rolls and he asks me to marry him
I swallow hard because I'm seven
and sleep with a stuffed giraffe named Gordo
when I cry for my daddy he sets up a mirror
then stands behind me and that's what I see
my daddy but all twisted up like he's dying
so I say I want to go home and they both say I am.

real problems

Gross, Gorgonzola

To my left a window, to my right a child.
And somewhere out that window is my other

child, down streets that wind to her school,
and other children down other lanes, and some
of them could have been mine, if I'd signed

or stood in line to foster or adopt, one could
be forking this same lettuce or saying, gross,

gorgonzola, and sitting between me
and the view of sad brown grass the sunlight
kicks through the window. If it grows

they could mow it, then spend
the pittance of their allowance on jujubes

at the movies which make their own
windows in dark caverns some distance
from mine, windows in which appear

still more children, whose lives
of magic or panic or spastic action

never happened, but mirror
the youths of scriptwriters and the empathies
of child actors, whose lives in turn

are weird and often come out sadly
as the lives of those unfostered kids

out there at some mysterious remove.
And if a window I once tried to hang by hand
had fallen differently, and sliced not my employer's

ankle but one of my own dear arteries,
if the shock had knocked me off the roof

to a jagged landing, then what would become
of this child on my right, in whom
windows open into vistas

of possibility, and I'm afraid
that in every passing minute another one

closes—I'm slow with the stick
to prop it, or fast with the word
to smash it, even as I say

stop playing with the cord, can't you see
I'm trying to type here, I hear a broom swish

to sweep up glass somewhere inside her,
and it's too late, when I ask how
were her carrots, and she asks for candy,

it's too late, but I say yes, help
yourself to some small thing.

Where The Orange Outlaw Is Hiding

It's in Jupiter's red spot
weathering methane and superlightning,
50 below zero, swirls
of frozen ammonia riffle
its pages, and my Megadeth shirt
is there, and the fence
that tore it, flat balls and bent
phones, a car seat with straps cut
and all the days the cat was gone,
and when the book sneaks out
(how? it's trapped
in a storm larger than the planet it ducked from)
when it sneaks out it slithers back into Jocelyn's
room to crumple the comics and hear the bedtime reading,
Nancy Drew tonight, all her favorite
books are mysteries
because in the end the vexing turns and questions
make sense, sudden deaths mood flashes
other people's brains things you hate and have to do
for no clear reason, and now that the book is
missing, the mystery
of the Orange Outlaw
will never be solved,
it will hang over lullabies and "things to think about"
although the book's brain is typed in paragraphs so it keeps
thinking about a stolen painting

a bowl of decimated citrus an orangutan
in fedora and trench coat
as it slinks back to its churning storm
while the girl missing the book
sleeps in hers, and wakes in hers, and goes to school in hers.

Watching My Daughter Learn to Skate at Veterans' Park

Jocelyn is splayed across the ice. Jocelyn is buckled into a black helmet too big for her head. Jocelyn spots me through the window, waves, then presses a mittened fist into the ice to push herself to standing. Wobbles on her skates, then thwacks happily onto her back. Between coat and snow pants she's got plenty of padding. It's cold out on the rink, so I hang back behind two panes of glass, taking care to laugh when I'm sure she's not looking.

I hang back behind two panes of glass, flipping through Amy Gerstler's *Dearest Creature*. Other mothers hold novels or notebooks. Other mothers are on cell phones. Gerstler tells a six-year-old niece about methods of execution from the encyclopedia (boiling, poisoning). It's a beautiful poem about the rebellions and lonelinesses of the very young, which strikes a chord given this creature inching across the ice, absolutely graceful in the seconds before her next flail and topple.

Other mothers are on cell phones. Despite trying not to eavesdrop, I hear "trouble presenting to adults" and "given his homosexuality." I hear "environment of domestic violence." I hear the practiced voice of a compassionate counselor. I pace in front of the glass and watch the ice; I put my face back in my book. I hear "made mistakes" and "first offense." I have no clear idea who she's talking to, or what about. I have tenuous ideas. They could be mistaken. They break me apart.

I put my face back in my book. A poem in the voice of a woman who left the 1893 World's Fair in Chicago on the arm of a serial killer. The voice of a ghost. So much can happen. The ice tilts under Jocelyn's skates. The ice rises up and smacks her flat. She's going to be so sore in the morning. What stunning luck.

Bullet with Your Name on It

When you are a preprinted address label,
you have no sense
of wonder or of time.
When the lid of a box
closes over your face,
and opens again,
that dark may fill four minutes
or forty years. Death
could be like that. When you are
a preprinted address label, nine-tenths of your personality
is fixed in early infancy—
your squat shape, dull finish, the birthmark
on your left side in the form of a precious orchid or
the UNICEF logo. You are born in makeup, tint and font
that inscribe for you one expression. In a window envelope
you arrive unbidden, an orphan dropped
on the doorstep among a colony of orphans,
tucked in with dire pleadings and a perforated
payment stub. You are less
than a dime a dozen. Peeled from a sheet, you reveal
a desperate, clingy side—once you're stuck,
you're stuck. Odds are you'll be bagged
with spoiled leftovers. Shredded. Incinerated.
You'll never make it out of the envelope. But suppose
you do: a practical thumb smoothes you in place to lend
the proper bureaucratic distance to

a holiday family newsletter. The deadest
of dead end jobs. Or suppose you are pressed upon
a skewed prayer bound
for a certain Francine in Topeka. She takes in
your poker face, sets the package on her palm
as if to weigh a memory.
Scrawls RETURN TO SENDER. Lets it clunk in the box.
And as the carrier delivers you back into the hand that sent you,
the instant you actualize your potential,
the man accepts his own package like a ticket
to a lonely grave. Better to lie
buried in a drawer with paper clips and ugly stationery
and the dim hope of being retrieved one day
by a child too young to discriminate among stickers.
A kid like that may smack you
to the handlebars of a tricycle. You soak up
a season of sprinkler mist, shouts of neighbors,
the fragrance of lawnmowers. Left
in the yard in a storm, cloudlight bleaches you blank
as droplets crash all around. And after the garage sale,
scraped away by new owners, you leave
a sticky patch on the bar no sponge
or sandpaper can scrub clean. Death could be
like that. Or instead she fastens you
in rings of red ink and glitter.
You brighten the fridge until you're taken down
to make space for a grocery list. The lid of a box
closes over your face, and opens again.
And there the man finds you,
red loops tangling over alphanumerics
as ivy would climb a headstone—

and in an instant his mind nails together
the house your digits plot,
fills it with lamplight and cinnamon.
He folds you into a package. He sends it to that house,
to a certain Francine in Topeka as if she's always been
there waiting for her childhood to
arrive and reopen in her hands,
as if death could ever be like that.

First Question

If your own gut starts to digest you. If your own blood
starves your engine. If the engine fails. If the ambulance
fails, scalpel fails, pill fails. The months of injections
that leave your nerves too threadbare to pick up a glass
of lemonade. You're dry erased. You tumble through
pain's trapdoor and the room fails, air fails, the trapeze
of branches shading the roof fails, and the chuffling sky,
the voice of the sky falls mute. Damn it, Dad. If your blood's
thicker than blood, shuts off the valve, if the pain doesn't
wake you, doesn't creep and flourish over hours, doesn't give
you time to wake and pop an aspirin and lay your numb
left arm over your chest, and stare, in the dark,
stare, get back up and pace and shake your wife and say
what you don't want to say. Hospital. Hurry. Because
to say it makes a map of the empty room and all its exits,
its lights that fail, its icicles melting from the eaves,
the unfed stray left pawing at the screens. But the house
is standing and someone will come back to it but if.
But only if. Say hospital. Get up. You've been opened
like this before. You've been dredged. Your upstart gut
meant to devour you. Your own cells. If you hadn't said
okay, colonoscopy, finally. Okay. And the scalpel.
Dramedies unspooled by portable DVD player
in the clinic for your three-hour drip every Tuesday
through a fall and a winter and a spring with DO NOT
TOUCH taped to the fridge and a city underwater

on the radio, helicopters passing over the populated
rooftops, their megaphones mute. Few by sky
are saved. Few are saved. Film rolls, a bicycle
with training wheels rolls down street whether you're there
to watch, or push, or not. If the trapdoor closes. I know.
It always closes. I've seen the ebony lid, the silver
rails, the lowering winch. I've handled the shovel.
No. Take the aspirin, climb in the car. If your
blood doesn't know better. Blood is stupid. Your gut
is stupid. You can't trust it, don't care what they say.
Say hospital. Say now. Lock the door behind you
when you leave the room empty, only that door,
the one for which you have a key. If your stupid
heart railroads you again. It's been a good
one but put your foot down. Wear the pants. Wear
the stupid blue gown, eat the beige mush they bring
on the cardiac tray. If a straw. If a bendy straw. Bend it.
Bend your lips to it. Wet them. Again. Wet them.

CHOPSTICKS

At five I learned to talk to women: "Hello
gorgeous," my aunt coached me
to greet her, and that was my repertoire
until these twiddly sticks plagued my fingers
on a dinner date. Embarrassed
to admit my hands didn't know how to behave
I stabbed and pinched like a cramped crab,
each morsel hovering an inch off the plate
then plunking back. Years of practice
to wield them before this gravity
in Mom's voice skews the phone
in my palm, and every syllable to say
falls away before I can wrap my mouth around it.
Les is dying again. Remission's in remission.
I've seen her clothes heaped on the edge of the tub,
wig on top, and thought for an instant she'd been
disintegrated. Now she has appointments
with blasts of light. She's scorched
through syringes and shrivels to a husk
so full of pain and morphine I wonder
what space is left inside. I can't find
a grip that could transfer a sliver of solace
through the foreign bones of her hand.
But later my mother will take up
that hand, and speak through fog,
gentle words that will ease Les out of pain,
simple as plucking the last scrap of her own heart
and lifting it to the night sky's open mouth.

And Then It Hits You:

one column ton of atmosphere driven down
on your shoulders, into each square foot of you,
from the obstetrician's slap to the door
that smacks you on the way out,

drizzle and zephyr, high five and face punch,
pat on or knife in the back, lips and wisps
of hair and whispers and whimpers, the hips of one
you think you're in love with, the hips of one you're sure

you'll never love, and maybe a feather, a riding crop,
cubes of ice and dollops of cream *and sudden harpsong*
as if the gathered clouds bounced dimes off your power lines
in perfect arpeggios, spraying notes which jangle the threads

in your sheets and gild the hairs on your arms, music
which makes your Olympian heart swim
to catch it before it dwindles, before it's drowned
in the high-pressure steam of a hot shower,

pumice and gel, aloe and the scrape
of a four-bladed razor, aerosol blasts of disinfectant
and germs nonetheless, spores, the force
of a sneeze, the tissue's gruff pulp,

the lashings of passing plants, their poisonous oils, bites
from mites, chiggers, fire ants, mosquitoes, horseflies,

dogs, a horse, a snapping turtle, jolts from circuits,
a skid past the guardrail, adrenaline, sugar,

prescription and nonprescription drugs, an embolism here,
an aneurysm there *and the ting and chime*
dirging overhead as if lightning played the dishes
and antennas like a carillon to sing you under the waves,

the distinctive brassglass sonics of a real live harp
you could be strung upon like that body of Bosch's,
fine wires shimmering with sound where it hurts worst
and the pummeling hands of the EMT, the defibrillator,

the hot flashlight roving your retina, 30 frames per second
crossing screens, magazine sheen, ultraviolet,
violets, vinegar, feedback shrieking
from a Marshall stack, the collapse of your cat,

your mother's stumble, the note left by your brother,
the obituary for your best friend, and your next
best friend, the table quake that brings down
your grand illusory structure of marshmallows and toothpicks,

the door you slam in your father's face echoing
back, your father's face slamming back, the earth, the enormity
of sky above and earth below pounding you
with every footfall, rumbling through

your cables and trusses, step by step and tick
by tick, until the day
you're broke and motionless
in the back of the library's green-paneled conference room

where a daughter you don't know
how to handle sits twenty feet from you listening
to the story of Jack and the Beanstalk,
and he's just doomed

himself and his mother to starve by trading their cow
for the beggar's beans, and his face rings red
with his mother's smack and his mother's names
as she tossed the beans out the window, and then

it hits you: you're Jack and this is your story,
you've arrived in the middle, as Jack lays awake
ruing his move and replaying his mother's rage
until he steps to the window with a rush of hope and sees

the yard chewed bare by the cow who is no longer
their cow, and the moonlit beans
not sprouting, and in the morning nothing, so he digs
and buries, waters and watches again at night

and sees nothing, night after night, except the furrows
deepening between his mother's ribs, until one day
the house is repossessed
and Jack and his mother beg in the streets,

they meet swindlers who try passersby
with the promise of magic
lug nuts, magic twigs, whatever they've shined up
from that day's trash, and it works, nets a coin

or egg in exchange, but never livestock, most wouldn't have
the audacity to ask, but Jack polishes cartons

and demands brocades from princes, and gets kicks,
and so his mother dies of hunger, and he's on the brink himself

as one day he passes the old house where the new gardener
is uprooting these crazy weeds from the flowerbeds,
and you think—how's this the story? how's there no ladder,
when your legs quake and seize

from the climb? where's that golden harp
you've heard in your head, percussion that sings,
as if pain itself should sing
if you held yourself at perfect angles to the barrage.

Elegy in Six Limericks

—for Spencer Miles Kimball

There was a young man of Ann Arbor
who was notably shy of the barber.
    While he'd calibrate phrases
    and navigate mazes
his bright beard grew to cover the harbor.

I say harbor implying a coastline,
though our town's in a midwestern ghost clime.
    We have water and air,
    frozen yogurt, despair,
but few sheltering shores where the boats line.

There were some old nerves who rang off-key.
I can't say if he slurped or spurned coffee.
    In so few ways I knew him
    but meant something to him.
When he harbored delights, he spoke softly.

There was an old man with a weapon
no substance or cease-fire could threaten.
    If you'd beg him, or scold him,
    if you loved him and told him,
it rose up inside him, against him.

We have stood by the earth where his flesh is.
We have studied his words and made guesses.
          Each few weeks I'm amazed
          at his dead Facebook page
with its offer: Send Spencer a Message.

I say harbor implying a boat.
I say earth where his flesh is a coat.
          Send Spencer a Message
          Send Spencer a Message
His beard grew to cover his throat.

Hologram for Ice and Axe

I.

The youngest suicide attempt I've seen
was four years old, says Rachel. Four years old.
What pincers struck? What spilled in that boy's brain
and hissed in swirling jets of pressured steam?
Some parent found him with a bedsheet coiled
around his neck by his own thumbs. Who called
him home? Almost too young to write his name
but not to scribble it out. The hand's too cold
around my beer but frozen to the glass.
I will not hear another word all night
though Rachel's Bellevue is far away (her face
looks tired) and we had come to celebrate.
Sheet clenched in palms still too uncreased to read.
Was it something that I said? That someone said?

II.

Was it something that I said? That someone sang
"I Hate Myself and Want to Die" then blew
apart the mesh that bound up all his school
is true. Is a fine kettle of fish. Bang.
I'd loved that river dredge of Kurt Cobain's
gray voice, the distress call bellows that chew
the ear from inside out. It's how I knew
the raucous bite-back force of aimless pain
before I ever—that's a lie. I'd stared
at days on end like a tunnel of zeroes
that mocked my worth. Kurt cut his nets and poured
forth all his fish toward what depths or shallows
in bloody shreds and bits. The diver chums
the ocean, gets whatever sharks may swim.

III.

The ocean gets whatever sharks may swim,
what drills may bore and burst and spew and spew.
A moon and magma tell it what to do.
One day my daughter said, "You know that cat song
about how 'a square with a horn
makes you wish you weren't born'?" I said I knew.
She'd croon it in the car, theme from a cartoon.
I sat on the bed. She didn't smile or frown.
"Well that's what I wish." Currents drive and rush
from hemisphere to crooked hemisphere.
The water doesn't hope, draw rein, or push;
a medium inherits what it can't repair.
Its depths are vast and dark. What could I have said
to snatch at lightning tucked inside her head?

IV.

To snap at lightning tucked inside our heads,
I'm told, is what psychologists are for.
There's a plastic dollhouse and a bulletin board
tacked full of crayoned pictures by other kids
who hate or bite themselves or wet their beds.
She'll say her name. Each time they ask for more
she sinks further into the couch, into floor.
She points at me to repeat the things she's said:
"I wish I wasn't alive." That was the first.
When I pressed the issue, she scoffed, "No, Dad"—
she wouldn't be sad to miss her tale's next twist
because "I wouldn't be alive to be sad."
More than I've ever been for my own sealed scars
I'm terrified of the brain's canisters and jars.

V.

I’m terrified of the brain’s canisters and jars,
their spring-loaded snakes, fangs packed with poison.
He’s licking a scoop of blue moon in the sun
with reasons to be happy: three or four
good friends, two prize submissions in the works,
a woman who loves him more than he could earn,
and bang—there goes another one,
venom staining his every past and future.
The week that Spencer choked down fifty pills
and survived (we thought) in tubes and deep sedation,
my daughter drew his face and scrawled, “get well,”
scribbled his red beard in fire, frustration.
He never woke to see it, that mouth agape,
left open to let the runts inside escape.

VI.

Left hanging wide to let out all the runts—
she's five and failed to get the back door shut.
You have to be more careful, she heard me shout.
Do you like worrying like this? I don't.
By the time we found and latched it—ten minutes?—
of course our quacking tailless manx got out.
We combed the neighborhood for hours on foot,
both tight with dread. We thought we spied him once.
Ten days the cat was gone. What guts me is this:
ninth night, her level gaze, so matter of fact
as she told the babysitter's smiling face,
"Ollie ran away. It was all my fault."
That's how the shouting echoes and may for years.
She hears it in her sleep: the fault is yours.

VII.

She hears it in her sleep: the fault is yours.
Eve is eleven. She's become the color blue
because that's what I asked the class to do.
She's become the scent of Colgate gel and fjords,
a blank lake cut with Evinrudes and storms.
Eve's a dancer. In her poem's twist, Blue knows
she's beautiful, but if one person says
he doesn't love her, that one pain devours
her utterly. "Autobiography,"
Eve calls it. I jot: "funny because it's true."
Next week she writes of chains, dead doves, her new
diagnosis of depression. Oh.
You're eleven. You're four. One day you wake up
and all the notes clang wrong and strangle hope.

VIII.

When all the notes clang wrong and strangle hope
my brother pulls his rig off of the road
and staggers from the cab. And leaves his load.
And leaves his livelihood. And dares not weep.
And takes a step and then another step
until the merchandise (not grief) he towed
has vanished, and he finds a working phone
and chants into it. Pick up. Please pick up.
The ringing splits my parents' darkened room.
"Oh Christ, what time is it?" They know it's him
in Syracuse. In Memphis. In Des Moines.
They've got the call a half a dozen times.
They drive all night to find their son astonished
at how his road gave out before it finished.

IX.

The why the hand gave out before it finished
is the survivors' theme. He was our son.
My god, what have we—what could we have—done?
They say depression can't be cured, just managed,
but that's not exactly true. Think of the courage
it takes to lay the barrel to your brain
or gulp the pills or dive off the garage.
The tidal courage it takes to refrain.
What gravity did we exert? We comb
through Spencer's effects. We read the note.
The love we parceled to him, did it worm
its way into these stanzas that he wrought?
Here's a bearing wall he left without a roof,
a page of broken markers trailing off.

X.

A page of broken markers trailing off
is what my daughter sees, learning to read.
She stutters through the cluster of a word,
its algebra of consonants and schwas,
then slumps or wails or hops down in a huff
and dashes for the dark side of the bed.
I climb the stairs to tell her that was good
until the Worry Bully got rough.
That's what we gained from two psychologists:
a hologram for the ice and axe she feels.
But she feels it. She's five, not stupid, so she blurts,
"Dad, the Worry Bully isn't real."
It's real and helpless, how we try to focus
the way her brain churns muck below the surface.

XI.

The way his brain churns muck below the surface
is what they ask in group time in the ward
with its jumbled jigsaw boxes and windows barred.
Sixth floor. My brother goes there when he's faceless,
when the inward roiling leaches all his substance
and leaves his eyes' horizons smoking, charred.
We cast and ask but cannot pull a word
from the whirlpool sucking him down, anxious, faithless.
Spencer'd done a stint there without pencils,
without razors or consent to his prescriptions,
without one unguarded moment at the urinal.
No headphones. (Wires are tools for strangulation.)
The nurses' every sentence spoken soft.
Each face's gentleness a master bluff.

XII.

Each face's gentleness a master bluff:
no confiding friend or doctor's mastery
can fathom my daughter. Her mind's a mystery
and not. Some afternoons she's plain enough,
bellows a sigh and says "I hate myself."
She can reach into the knife drawer easily.
We fill the tub for her then step away,
can't bear to trust the words. But the breath beneath
we count on. There's more the body wants
than what the neural lightning welds or charges.
I take her in my lap. I take her hands.
I will an outward brightness, though my urge is
to squeeze and rail and rocket her from sadness.
Our panics clutch at love and chance with absence.

XIII.

Our panics clutch at love and charge at absence,
they race through yards after a live black blur.
What have I done to, or for, my daughter?
Like a fairy tale king, I hear the sentence
pronounced against her and rage to banish
spindles from the kingdom. We spotted fur,
out searching that day, and I turned from her
and dashed after the cat. She watched me vanish.
She stood in the world alone, shaking or still,
as I did my idiot best to help, and screwed
up worse, chased what she'd loosed from home for good.
She stood alone in the world and always will.
Who wouldn't flail at loss, who wouldn't love
to refuse that it could loom as a relief?

XIV.

To refuse that it could loom as a relief,
this yawning blank, from one's own ghost-kicked brain
is lunacy we depend on. We think pain
should show in scars or a case file thick with griefs
but no. Nor trauma nor logic. A toddler coughs
as they loosen the sheet from his neck and demand,
why? Why does my daughter squeeze her hands
and bang them into her own chest and face?
Was it nothing that I said? And if not,
is there nothing I can say to take it back?
No one can guess how real or permanent
her hopelessness could be. The tongue is stuck
for prayers or prescriptions to spare her being
the youngest suicide attempt I've seen.

XV.

The youngest suicide attempt I've seen
was something that I said that someone said.
The ocean gets whatever sharks may swim
to snap at lightning tucked inside our heads.
I'm terrified of the brain's canisters and jars
left open to let the runts inside escape.
She hears it in her sleep: the fault is yours
that all the notes clang wrong and strangle hope.
The way that hand gave out before it finished
a page of broken markers trailing off—
and how that brain churned muck below the surface,
the face's gentleness a master bluff—
our panics clutch at love and chance with absence
to refuse that it could loom as a relief.

Things to Think About

—for Zoe

Not fire. Not fire cascading in blue jewels
    from the stovetop gas jets, not tentacling
the tile, not fire creaking up the stairs, trying on the clothes
    in your closet. Not fire twining like ivy
up your mother's bones. Saying not fire,
    though, is the same as saying fire, nebulas
of gasoline, starbursts in the soap dish,
    magma running in the gutters.

You've never seen a blaze not caught
    behind a grill or sunk inside a circle of stones,
never seen a spark catch a curtain
    or race along a fuse but in your head
dust is gunpowder and your body wrapped in sheets
    a mummy in a furnace, so if you're not thinking
about Athena being born wearing armor,
    of the clank when she lands on her feet

and turns, armed, to face her father's gaping brain,
    think of snails at the shell wash,
a burger joint in the basement.
    Think of cloudboats or whaleboats
or a sun with no fire in it, just continually opening
    daffodils pouring nectar over the planets.

Think of things you can send in an envelope,
things you can lead on a leash.

Think of what the sun could be made of
if it wasn't fire, not fire licking its chops,
breathing in your ear as you sleep,
saying shh, don't wake up, it's all in your head,
and it is, the fire, it's all in your head,
you can kill it with a thought, so think
of all the things you could build a bridge from
for your tubful of plastic people,

think of the plots of puppet shows for pandas,
think of when you and I used to dance
to Mr. Jack, how we stomped and thrashed around the purple
swivel chair as a voice screamed Fuck! You! Pig!
though you were three and didn't catch it
and your memory of those years is burnt clean,
everything burns, everything will,
but if you let that thought overtake you as you lie

in the dark we're half ash already,
so think of the bridge you'll build
and the township waiting for your people on the other side
with turquoise pools and a lean-to
made of picture books, think of the fabulous animals
with whom they'll talk about the view
across the river of the smoking quarry they have left behind,
its veins of charcoal, its glorious ores.

Acknowledgments

Many thanks to my family and friends, and especially to Karrie Waarala, Fiona Chamness, Jeanann Verlee, Julie Babcock, Jeff Kass, Marianne Boruch, Alice Fulton, David Kirby, and J.A. Tyler for their generous attention to this collection.